I BEAT THE ODDS

There's Hope And Healing For You

I BEAT THE ODDS

There's Hope And Healing For You

Maureen L. Whitsett

Published by:
Queen of the Keys Publishing
10045 Baltimore National Pike, Ste A7 #1144
Ellicott City, Maryland 21042
https://queenofthekeyspublishing.com

ISBN: 979-8-9939071-0-9

Contact Maureen Whitsett or invite her to speak at your next engagement:
Email: maureen@thequeenofthekeys.com

Editor: Maletta P. Simmons

Printed in the United States of America, 2026

Disclaimer:
This book was written to provide hope and healing. My prayer is that you will be inspired to seek the help you need in your unique situation. I am not a doctor, therapist, or licensed counselor. I am an author who has overcome life's challenges with the help of God Almighty, and I share my experiences to encourage, uplift, and offer hope and healing to others.

Dedication

Giving honor to God, my Lord, and Savior Jesus Christ, I am incredibly happy to be alive today and to pen this book to help others. I love God so much. I thank you, Heavenly Father for being my protector when I could not protect myself. Thank you for being there with me during every hospital stay. I could not have made it without you.

I dedicate this book to my three adult daughters Maletta Simmons, Melony Pritchett, and Maureen Pritchett. I love these beautiful ladies. They have grown to be such a blessing to my life. I must say, they bring out the kid in me with much laughter. These ladies have been my life and I thank God for them.

Thank you to my special friend, Dr. Dawn Harvey-Owens. You have a special place in my heart. I'm grateful to God for all that you mean to me and my family.

Loving Endorsement

There are no words to describe how proud I am of my mom. Not only does it take a lot of courage to fight for your life, but it also takes a lot of strength as well. I believe that God gave my mom a double dose as He knew that she would need it on her life journey.

Not only am I a survivor of having a teenage mom, but I am also a survivor of having a mom with mental health challenges. My mom is not the only one that Beat the Odds!!

Maletta P. Simmons

Table of Contents

Maureen

Spiritual Connotation: BELOVED

Scripture: Psalm 139:17-18 (The Living Bible)
How precious it is, Lord, to realize that you are thinking about me constantly! I can't even count how many times a day your thoughts turn toward me. And when I waken in the morning, you are still thinking of me!

Adorned by God

Scripture: Isaiah 61:10-11 (The Message)
I will sing for joy in GOD, explode in praise from deep in my soul! He dressed me up in a suit of salvation, he outfitted me in a robe of righteousness, As a bridegroom who puts on a tuxedo and a bride a jeweled tiara. For as the earth bursts with spring wildflowers, and as a garden cascades with blossoms, So the Master, GOD, brings righteousness into full bloom and puts praise on display before the nations.

Introduction – A Book Of Hope And Healing For You

This book has been inside of me for many years. My oldest daughter, Maletta Simmons asked me, during the chaotic worldwide Coronavirus (COVID-19), what projects are you going to be working on. I had two answers, I had moved six months earlier and was taking my time unpacking boxes. I said I would unpack my boxes and write my book. She said good. Incidentally, Maletta has been with me through thick and thin and has witnessed a lot of my perplexing experiences that I'm going to share with you in this book. Before I go any further, I want to take time out to thank her, Thank you, Maletta! All of my daughters are special, but I wanted to say thank you to Maletta. We're about to turn the corner into 2022. I started my book in April of 2020. I would start and stop writing on so many occasions, never finishing. I've purposed to keep going this time at age 60 until I get finished. I have no more excuses since recently retiring on September 30, 2021. YaY!!

I have been through some seasonal traumatic experiences. I thank God, that He has brought me into His rest by His grace and mercy. My prayer for writing this book is that it will bring you hope and start your journey to enter into the rest of God. *(Deuteronomy 25:19, 1 Chronicles 23:25, and 2 Chronicles 20:30)* Please read these scripture references. Choose the version of the Bible that speaks to your heart. My purpose in sharing this book is to bring you hope and healing. I also want to plant a seed just like my grandmother planted a seed in me many years ago. I didn't know I would need Jesus Christ, but I really needed Him. Jesus was there for me every time. So grateful, for the mercy and grace that was shown to me.

My prayer is, whatever you may be facing during this season of your life that you have faith in God to bring you through. There's an old song titled, "Hold on to God's Unchanging Hand." This song is sung by some prominent gospel artists. I particularly like the version sung by the Chicago Mass Choir. It's worth a listen.

Come on this journey with me. As you see, the name of this book is, ***"I Beat The Odds – There's Hope And Healing For You."*** Have you ever had some things against you? While I tell my story, my hope is to encourage you on how you can beat the odds in your own life.

Chapter 1 – The Early Days
(5-9 Years Old)

My friend and I were supposed to be playing outside in the projects of Washington, DC. I was only about five years old. I found myself entering the grocery store with her. We started eating food we had not purchased. It was the first time I remember being in a grocery store without my mother. The concept of eating food without paying for it didn't cross my little five-year-old mind. I was with my friend and thought it was ok. A security guard took both of us to a room and we waited for a long time. The next thing I knew my mother was there. We went home and I'm not sure what the punishment was, but I know there was screaming and hollering between my mother and father.

I have two older siblings (one is deceased now) and one younger brother. I have another brother who was born when my mother was older but not during this timeframe. There were times when my sister, brothers, and I were asked to go outside. Those were the times my father would abuse my mother. I remember my mother crying at times. My father was also an alcoholic. I was too young to really understand what was going on.

I did have one fond memory during this timeframe of my life. The hill in the back of our house was the sole source of enjoyment when it snowed. For hours we would slide down on cardboard boxes that we used as sleds, it was so much fun.

The next thing I knew my brothers and sister and I were living with my grandmother in South Carolina. Mrs. Violet Vernon is deceased and was widowed for some years, I have come to appreciate her after 62 years of living. My mom literally ran away from my biological father when I was five years old. I never saw him again. I was too young to understand Domestic Violence. My mother did what she had to do.

Chapter 2 – The God Of My Grandmother
(The Seed Of God Being Planted)

I have fond memories of living with my grandmother in South Carolina. She was a tough Christian woman, who has gone on to glory. She lived until she was 91 years old.

When she told you to do something and if you did not hear her the first time you were in big trouble. My grandmother did not use a belt, we broke off plenty of switches from the trees in her yard. If I played in my church clothes, there was a beating coming from the switch. I learned very early not to play in my church clothes.

I remember at 6 years old, singing in the children's choir, one song in particular, "Jesus loves me this I know, for the Bible tells me so." That was a defining moment for me in my life and I didn't know it. There was a spiritual seed being planted within me that I would need as I endured some stormy and traumatic experiences in my life.

My purpose in sharing my story is to give you "Hope" and I pray for everyone who reads this book to be "Healed" from whatever situation they find themselves in, or have been in. God is fully aware of it ALL; you may not think anything is happening in your life because you cannot see it with your natural eyes, believe me, even when you can't see it, God is always moving.

I learned about God and His Son, Jesus Christ by attending church with my grandmother, by the way, it was an all-day event. The seed that was planted in my spirit during those early years of my life would be the anchor for my soul to carry me for many years to come and even now. I am incredibly grateful for that seed being planted. When my siblings and I would sit with my grandmother in church if you talked or fell asleep, you got the biggest pinch of your life. Boy did those pinches hurt and my grandmother dared you to cry in church. My children have similar stories, as those pinches were passed down to them. By attending church with my grandmother, the pinches kept me straight and I wanted my children to be just as straight when they were with me in church. I was learning about continuing the legacy of my grandmother while having a relationship with the Lord Jesus Christ without really knowing what I was doing. It just felt natural.

My grandmother was a matriarch. I was told that she has a wing of the church dedicated to her where she taught Sunday School. As God would have it, I've taught Sunday School on occasion.

We had to work in the summertime picking peaches. That was a difficult time for me because I was from the city. When we lived with our mother we had chores in the house, but I never had a job until I got to my grandmother's house. I was not that tall; I was around seven years old by this time and had to pick peaches from a tree. There were lots of peach orchards in the South. You had to wear layers of clothes, so the peach fuzz did not get on your skin. If the peach fuzz landed on your skin, it made your skin very itchy. Once the sun came up it was extremely hot outside, and the humidity was unbearable. On many occasions, my older sister would help me fill my baskets with peaches so I could get tickets. The tickets would convert into money at the end of the day. We picked peaches every summer I remember so we could purchase clothes before school started. My grandmother didn't work outside her home, but she had vegetable gardens of all sorts. I remember breaking string beans into small pieces, and shucking corn, etc. Some of you reading this are probably wondering what is "shucking corn?" When shucking corn, you peel off the outer leaves, grasp the tops of the leaves and the tassels, pull down in one firm tug, then break off the leaves and the silks, pluck off any remaining pieces of the silk, and repeat. I had a good example of work ethic inside and outside of the home.

I remember the family reunions when all our families near and far would come to Grandma's house in South Carolina. My grandmother had 14 children, nine boys and five girls. I would play with my cousins and eat great country food. The food today does not taste at all like the food tasted back in my grandma's day. Life was so good!

When I was nine years old, my mother got a house that we could call our home in the state of Maryland, so we settled there as a family. Again, life was good, no more peaches to pick. I played hard; I followed in my big brother's footsteps everywhere he went I wanted to go. If he went to play basketball, I went. If he went outside to play street football, I was there too. Again, life was good with no cares in the world.

Chapter 3 – The Molestation. Why?
(10-12 Years Old)

A report of child abuse is made every 10 seconds, according to the American Society for the Positive Care of Children; 1 in 3 girls and 1 in 7 boys will be sexually assaulted by the time they reach 18, according to the Department of Justice; more than 4 children die each day because of child abuse, according to the U.S. Department of Health and Human Services.

More than 90% of child sexual abuse victims know their attacker; ("Sexual Assault of Young Children as Reported to Law Enforcement" by Howard Snyder). Approximately 70% of children that die from abuse are under the age of 4; (U.S. Department of Health and Human Services).
About 30% of abused and neglected children will later abuse their children, continuing the cycle of violence; (U.S. Department of Health and Human Services).

In terms of the above statistics, "I Beat the Odds." I didn't die even though on many days as an adult survivor of child sexual abuse, I felt so much like dying because of the pain I was in, "I Beat the Odds." I didn't abuse my children, "I Beat the Odds." There was no cycle of domestic violence, "I Beat the Odds." To God be all the glory! The believers in Jesus Christ will understand how my beating the odds with the help of the Holy Spirit broke generational curses. Amen!

In my early childhood, before age 10, I was so happy, I enjoyed my family, and my extended family, and the world was good. It was wonderful as I remember it. When we were very young, my mother did the best she could with four children.

My first traumatic experience happened when I was only 10 years old and my whole world changed forever. I was sexually abused and didn't understand what happened or what was going on. Today, I understand from a Spiritual perspective I was targeted to be destroyed early in my life by Satan. Why do I say that? It wasn't until I entered Junior High School that I understood what had really happened in that bedroom. I was a victim of childhood sexual abuse. I developed anxieties, became depressed, I felt violated, and I was no longer a happy little girl. The person that was supposed to protect me didn't. The sexual abuse was never reported. The normalcy of my life continued to change year after year. It is an unwritten rule in most African American households, if we were not told verbally, we knew that what goes on in the house stayed in the house. I know most of us have secrets. Sometimes, freedom is getting those secrets out. Secrets are not always comfortable to reveal. There should be a purpose in revealing your secret(s). There were ramifications for holding on to my secrets. The secret ate at my insides and distorted my view of people and my world. The happy little girl that I was before 10 years old, started disappearing even though I was visible to others. I stuffed the memory of my first traumatic experience *(being sexually abused)* deep into my subconscious. Even though the flashbacks were there, I did what I could to move on. The sadness started as I relived the experience over and over in my mind, asking myself "Why."

I would cling to my oldest brother, who is now deceased. I would tag along with him as a tomboy *(a girl who enjoys rough, noisy activities traditionally associated with boys)*. I was hiding behind the feminine part of me. I played basketball and football with him and his friends. It brought me so much happiness. He was my hero. Time went on and my brother went off to the Army. When he returned, he was not the same. I don't know what he experienced or seen; he never shared them with me. But we never got that relationship back that we had before he left for the Army. I missed our relationship so much.

Researchers estimate that police only receive reports of 1% to 10% of all sexually abused children. Many factors influence this widespread trend of underreporting, such as intimidation, social stigmas, and other societal pressures.

Child sexual abuse opens the door for all manner of serious issues later in life that can include mental illness, poor socialization, substance abuse, and even fatal diseases. Victims need to speak up about their experiences and strive to hold their abusers accountable. Children are often incapable of understanding these situations, so it's up to parents to stay vigilant and notice any strange behavioral changes in their children.

Chapter 4 – A Teenage Mother
(Fast Forward, Age 16)

At age 15, I met my soon-to-be husband, who became my best friend, confidant, and my whole world. He was considerably older than I was by seven years. He passed away at the age of 59. We became very good friends and developed a bonding relationship. I became part of the rising statistics in the 70's, a teenage mother at 16 years of age out of wedlock. Studies have shown that sexual precocity (a child's physical signs of sexual maturity develop too soon). Precocious puberty happens before age 8 in girls, and before age 9 in boys. Signs can include breast growth, pubic hair, and voice changes. This in combination with sexual abuse, was related to much higher incidences of teenage pregnancy, according to the Journal of Marriage and Family.

I didn't think I had signs of sexual precocity. Now that I look back years later and understand body language, I feel, I was sending signals unknowingly of wanting someone to protect me; because the person that was supposed to be my protector did not. After I had my second daughter we were married. Our third daughter came along four years later. It was a short marriage of seven years.

It was 1975, my oldest daughter Maletta had not been born yet. Our bonding and friendship developed quickly. He had a large afro and liked to get his hair braided so when he picked it out it stood fresh and neat. *(If you were born after the '70's, you may not know the term pick. It was a type of comb that made your hair go straight out into a bush. Bush, another term used in the 70's).* As a favor for braiding his hair, he said he would take me to McDonald's. The Big Mac in the 1975 era, was compared to Filet Minon at Ruth Chris, The Steak House of today. When the adults in that era wanted to treat their families, McDonald's was the place to go. McDonald's food tasted much better back in the 70's. McDonald's was the place to take your families and it was a treat. As a way to return the favor for braiding his hair, whenever I wanted to go to McDonald's he would take me. I was so ecstatic, oh my goodness. McDonald's here we come! That was the best! At first, I thought I was just braiding his hair, it was fine it was cool. But the more and more time we spent together I realized that he was such a nice person. He was nice to everyone. He had relocated to my neighborhood from Chicago, IL., and lived right next door to us. He was a good-looking young man too.

In 1975, mentoring wasn't a buzzword like it is today, but he was mentoring my friends that I played football and basketball with. He was a sports fanatic. He enjoyed teaching us. I was out with the boys along with my oldest brother and learning as well. I enjoyed it!! I don't know when the shift happened, but somewhere it happened. I started looking at my friend more than just a friend while he was teaching us how to play sports. When the shift happened; wow, I found myself trying to figure out when to skip high school. Let me say, I did finish high school. He even helped at times with my high school homework. We were so close and inseparable. Soon after, in the last year of high school, I had my oldest daughter. He was there for me; he was in the delivery room. He attended the Lamaze classes with me. It was not popular to be pregnant at age 15. When I had my oldest daughter Maletta in 1977, I was 16 years old. All the expectations you would have from a gentleman, he was that and more. He brought my high school clothes. I mean he purchased $60.00 jeans, more than one pair, and my entire wardrobe in 1975. It was interesting, he spoiled me, and he was my best friend. I shared everything with him. As soon as I graduated from high school, I was immediately encouraged and wanted to go to college. I stayed home during the day with my oldest daughter and *(we were not married at this time; we didn't get married until our second child was born)*; he would stay home with her while I went to evening college. But, when I walked into the room on my first day of evening college, everyone in the room was old enough to be my parent, what a disaster. It was a culture shock for me, and it was something I tried to do, but I couldn't manage it at my age. I eventually decided to go to work. Later on, I would stumble into a clerical program. As long as you passed the clerical program, which was very intense, they would place you in government employment. I did go back to college several times during my adult life. I did not receive a degree in book knowledge, but I did receive a master's degree in life itself.

Because I was molested at an incredibly young age, I could not fully accept my husband's love for me. Studies show that sexual trauma may make a person feel unloved or unworthy of love, feeling that no one will ever accept them and treat them well. (https://vantagepointrecovery.com/past-sexual-trauma/#) (vantagepointrecovery.com, n.d.)

The relationship before we were married and after we were married would have many dynamics, he would operate as a dad to me, my boyfriend, or my husband, or a combination of the three at different times. There was never any domestic violence in our relationship. Thank God!! But I did feel controlled and that was because I never matured before I had my children, and I hadn't dealt with the emotional and mental challenges I had. Also, by this time, his parents had relocated from Chicago, IL, and lived with us and that experience is shared later in the book. Nevertheless, after a while, I resented the controlling element and rebelled. Especially, after his parents had lived with us for a considerable amount of time. Everything got to be too much, the marriage and his parents in the home with us. His parents finally moved out. I thought our marriage would get better, but it didn't. I rebelled and dated outside of my marriage and my husband found out. We had two children by this time. He left me and I went back home to my mother's house.

Chapter 5 – Losing My Way
(The Little Girl)

I left my mother's home and moved in with my soon-to-be husband when my oldest daughter Maletta was 15 months old and the only child at the time. I was not healed and had not been going to church nor did I continue to cultivate my relationship with Jesus Christ that my grandmother had introduced me to. I was losing my way.

During our relationship and after we were married these were the things I experienced because I know now that I needed to be healed from all that I had been through.

- Outside interference from our parents
    - I would say that this was the biggest challenge. The outside interference came from both our parents, and this was not fun.
- Father-daughter relationship instead of a husband-and-wife relationship
    - We really cared for each other, and he wanted to take care of me, but I was very wounded from the traumatic experiences.
- Teenager with adult responsibilities
    - When I became a teenage mother, I had to grow up quickly, e.g., running a household, having a husband, and

trying to be a woman, but not knowing how to take care of myself as a woman.

- Sexual problems
  - If you've ever experienced being sexually abused, some scars are not visible to the naked eye, and it'll take the grace of God for your healing and lots of communication with your spouse to overcome. I didn't have the communication skills to talk this through.
- Moving back home many times
  - My mom's house became a revolving door for me and my children. When things didn't go right with the marriage, I found myself at my mother's house. Because I was not mature during these times, it created lots of problems.
- Lack of communication
  - Again, the lack of maturity and lack of communication skills for marriage was to my detriment.

As I look back over this critical time in my life, I could have used a very good counselor. Going to a counselor was not popular in the 70's. Having a positive church home would have also been key. Positive is the "operative word." You don't want people taking sides but sharing the truth with both parties in love.

I had a lot of little girl tendencies because I believe that in a sense, I stopped maturing into a woman when the sexual abuse happened. I stopped maturing at age 10 and because I didn't deal with the issues it caused me to later spiral out of control. The pain would be so unbearable that eventually, I would implode. Implode, is a person subjected to intense pressures who, emotionally at least, bursts inward. I would receive certified counseling later in life, but not during this time.

I am a true fan of positive certified counseling. It will do wonders for your communication skills as well as teach you how to confront others. The scriptures say, *"Where no counsel is, the people fall: but in the multitude of counsellors there is safety." (Proverbs 11:14 KJV)*. Boy, did I need safety and positive certified counsel?

Chapter 6 – The Perfect Syndrome
(Learning To Operate In Excellence And Not In Perfection)

Keeping the molestation, a secret at age 10 and well into my 20's consumed me and caused me to operate in a way that everything I did had to be perfect. Being perfect back then allowed me, I thought, to control the world around me since I could not control my world at age 10. But little did I know my world would still come crashing down around me.

There is a difference now in my thinking, to operate in excellence and not in perfection. I've been through a lot, and thank God, He's still healing me. I'm here to be all that God has created me to be. In the meantime, I'm hoping what I have been through can help others.

The sadness continued right through my early 20's after the sexual abuse. My girls were my world, and I had a great husband who was very understanding and patient. But I was not a happy person deep down inside. My husband knew about my sexual abuse and did everything he could to help me deal with it. He also knew the person who was responsible for allowing the sexual abuse to happen. He disliked the person, of course. That unresolved issue of sexual abuse tormented me most of my adult life. At that time, I was not thinking about forgiveness. I did not start going back to church until I was about 26 years old. It was still years later before I could forgive the person. I continued to ask myself "Why" did this person who was supposed to protect me allow the sexual abuse to happen? While it chipped away at me it affected my marriage even though my husband had a lot of patience. We also had interference from our mothers which didn't help our situation. After years of breaking up and getting back together, I finally asked for a divorce. Not because I wanted to, but because I could not deal with myself, and knowing I was broken into so many pieces, I thought it would ease the pain. Each time my daughters turned 10 years old, I relived the experience I went through again and again, how could this person allow this to happen to a 10-year-old child? It was agonizing at times. If you've never been violated, you cannot begin to understand or imagine the pain this causes even years later. It affects people differently. When it happened to me and you're introduced to sex in the manner I was, it was a very perplexing situation. At that age, I didn't understand what was happening, and I didn't know what to say to the person who was supposed to love and protect me. These feelings escalated as I got older.

If you have been violated, I understand you. I want you to be healed. I am a survivor and want to help others with hope and healing. I have put some resources in this book. If you need immediate help, please contact the resources I've shared in the Appendix. You can also reach out to see a certified counselor, or therapist, or call a trusted friend that will walk with you through this process of healing.

Chapter 7 – Journal Pages
(Your Thoughts Are Important, Journal What's On Your Heart)

I have shared a lot. Please, I want to encourage you to start talking to God through your writing with a sincere heart. It is a healing process that helped me tremendously throughout the years. You can make this your safe space. Journal what's on your heart. You can start with your early days. If you had a great early start to your life, journal about those great days. If you need to be healed from your early days, journal, then ask God to heal you. This is between you and God. God hears every prayer and puts every tear in a bottle. (Psalm 56:8 TLB – the entire Chapter is really comforting; I encourage you to read it). If you find you are running out of space, please get a journal notebook, or add blank pages and continue.

Chapter 8 – Life In Denial
(Not Realizing I Was In Denial)

This was a very touchy season for me around 1988. After a series of traumatic events, I did not understand what was happening to me. I went to several doctors, and one of the conditions I was told I had was major depression. One doctor said you will have to take medication for the rest of your life. What a blow to my intellect. How did I get here, I asked myself. No, the doctors must be wrong. I am not depressed, I'm just sad because I am still dealing with why I was molested at age 10. Doesn't anybody understand what I'm going through?

My sister would attempt to help me on different occasions while I was in my 20's. I was staying with her and her children during this point in my life. I vaguely remember this one situation when I got in my car and started driving. I don't recall having a destination. My sister had no clue where I was. She went outside to look for me and ran into a woman that she didn't know. The woman helped her to look for me and they found me in a parking lot sitting inside my car. My sister and I have always said that the woman must have been an angel that God sent to help her find me.

Even though I needed help, I insisted that I wasn't depressed and didn't need medication. This went on for several years. Again, forgiveness was the furthest thing from my mind. Every day my situation was getting worse. While I was in this season of my life, my sister would come to rescue me several times when I found myself in various situations. My younger brother was there for me as well.

After a while, no one knew how to help me. God had me holding on.

I believe by faith that in my many years of pursuing and crying out for deliverance and healing in my mind, by faith, Jesus touched me. I was just as determined as the woman who had a flow of blood for twelve years and came from behind and touched the hem of Jesus' garment. *For she said to herself, "If only I may touch His garment, I shall be made well."* Jesus turned around to the woman who suffered 12 years, and said, *"Be of good cheer, daughter; your faith has made you well." And the woman was made well from that hour. (Matthew 9:20-22 NKJV)* I'm not perfect, and just so you know, no one walking this earth is perfect. Only Jesus Christ is perfect. The more I grow by pressing toward the mark of the High Calling in Christ Jesus according to *Philippians 3:14 (TLB)* I am being made well. With the help of the Lord Jesus Christ and the fact that I'm still here, I beat the odds by His grace and mercy! I don't care how long you've been in pain in any way, you can beat the odds too! If you're in need of healing, the scriptures say all you need is faith as a grain of mustard seed. If you've ever seen the size of a mustard seed, it is extremely tiny. God says, your faith can be as small as a grain of mustard seed, and nothing will be impossible for you. If you need healing it is possible, hold on and receive by faith and trust God. *(Matthew 17:20 NKJV)*

Chapter 9 – The Scars Of Life
(Visible And Nonvisible Scars)

Webster defines scars (noun) as a mark left on the skin or within body tissue where a wound, burn, or sore has not healed completely, and fibrous connective tissue has developed. *"a faint scar ran down the length of his/her left cheek"* (verb) mark with a scar or scars. *"he/her is likely to be **scarred for life** after injuries to his face, arms, and legs".*

If we would be honest everyone has scars from this life, we live. Some have visible scars and others have scars that are not visibly detected.

I suffered with non-visible and now visible scars, only God could have brought me through such traumatic experiences. My non-visible scars started at the age of 10 but the manifestation that I was scarred didn't register to me until my teenage years before I was pregnant with my first daughter. Keeping the secret of the sexual abuse buried within me had the appearance of me being scarred for life. It was killing me slowly. Thank God for my grandmother and being introduced to Jesus Christ at the early age of 6 years old. I honestly believe that if I was not introduced to Jesus Christ at such an early age, I have no idea where I would have ended up in my life's journey. God's word says, *"train up a child in the way he should go and when he is old, he will not depart from it"* (Proverbs 22:6 KJV). At every low point in my life, when I needed to lean on God, He was there every time to pick me up. God is still here today to bring me out of the storms of life I still experience at times. And He's there for everyone who calls on Him. Jeremiah chapter 32, verse 17 talks about how nothing is too hard for God.

My visible scars took some getting used to. I am still faced with my visible scars when meeting new people. I am normally a shy person anyway until I get to know you then I open up. I do better with one-on-one conversations. Sometimes, if I'm out and about when people are looking at me, I say to myself what are they looking at and I must remember, they're looking at my scars.

My visible scars came as an attempt to take my own life. The pain I was experiencing was unbearable during this season in my life. If you have never been in a state of pain that's unbearable, you have no idea what this pain feels like. I've heard people say, no one should ever think about taking their own life. Unless you've been in a state of complete unrest in your mind, you have no idea what this pain feels like and please don't judge the people, but get them the help they need. Yes, I had my children to think about and my extended family. It wasn't a selfish act it was an act of attempting to free myself from the pain going on within my mind. I don't wish this pain on no one. I'm always deeply saddened when I hear of people who have taken their life by death to suicide. I understand them. It's the pain on the inside of them that they can no longer live with. They no longer have the hope to keep going. I am not giving permission to those who have lost hope to take their life. I am saying, I understand. There's hope and healing for you.

Attending a Bible-believing church where the love of God is shared with action will help your process and give you the hope you need to carry on. Also, getting qualified therapy or certified counseling can assist with your healing. You must be open-minded. You don't always need a crowd to go with you to therapy or counseling. Therapy/counseling can be healing just for you. Being in denial that you need the help will not help you or your situation.

The enemies of our lives (anything that wants to steal, kill, or destroy us) *(John 10:10 NKJV)*, will try to destroy us by any means necessary, but God! It's so vital that you understand how important it is to have a personal relationship with Jesus Christ. Not just for you, but for your family, those closest to you, and those coming behind you. If you can't be the one to lead your family and friends to Jesus Christ, pray that God would send those who they respect, and know Jesus Christ as their personal Savior to lead your family and friends to have their own personal relationship with Jesus Christ. As we read earlier, Jesus came so that we might have life and have life more abundantly *(John 10:10 KJV)*. Jesus is our life insurance, and no matter what comes our way, we're sure to come out on top. I'm a living witness to this testament. There are so many references to this truth in the scriptures. In Deuteronomy 28:1-68 the Message version, the scriptures show us the good if we listen to God and the bad if we do not listen to

God. My prayer is that whether you have visible or non-visible scars you have a desire to be a good listener when it comes to God.

Whether you currently have visible or non-visible scars, God is here to give you hope and healing. No matter what you are going through or have gone through to get the scars, *(Psalm 17:5-9 Amplified Bible)* are comforting scripture references.

v.5-My steps have held closely to Your paths; My feet have not staggered.

v.6-I have called upon You, for You, O God, will answer me; Incline Your ear to me, hear my speech.

v.7-Wondrously shows Your [marvelous and amazing] lovingkindness, O Savior of those who take refuge at Your right hand From those who rise up against them.

v.8-Keep me [in Your affectionate care, protect me] as the apple of Your eye; Hide me in the [protective] shadow of Your wings

v.9-From the wicked who despoil and deal violently with me, My deadly enemies who surround me.

Chapter 10 – There's Hope In God
(Don't Ever Lose Your Hope)

There will be days when you must encourage yourself. You can call someone, but that will not always be the answer. You can go out with your friends, but that will not always be the answer. Having hope in God and spending time with God will always be your answer. Here are several ways, as a suggestion, you can spend time alone with God, e.g., meditate on God's Word, even if you don't understand everything that you're reading, God will help you understand when it's time; listening to Gospel or Christian music, sometimes instrumental music is good too. Also, sitting quietly and thinking about all the things that you're grateful for that God has done. Being grateful can do wonders for uplifting your spirit. If you're reading this book, you're alive today and you're breathing. This is a great start to being grateful that you're alive! Social media is really big now since the pandemic. But I encourage you to take regular breaks from social media as it can be very addictive. I could go on and on, but you know what you've been through. And guess what, you're still here by the grace of God. God is almighty, God is the great I am, God is our God, God is our peace, God is our provider, God is in control, God created the heaven and earth, and God created you and me. God knows your blueprint; what you're made of on the inside. God knows what you're made of because He designed you before you were even thought of by your parents. *(Jeremiah 1:5 KJV)* God will always be there for you. Why? Because God is in control, and He has the whole world in His hands.

Having hope in God is having patience with yourself. Yes, the hardships and sufferings will come, but if we endure, it works patience in us. *(Romans 5:3 KJV and James 1:3 NKJV)*. We cannot avoid the hardships, nor can we avoid the sufferings. These challenges allow us to mature, improve, or expand our life in God. We sometimes will never know what we can handle until we go through the hardships and sufferings. If we're not tested in areas of our lives, we will never know if we can overcome the challenges. As hard as it seems, we're stronger when we get through our hardships and sufferings. And we can say, "God Did It!" God will always do it because He's that type of God. A faithful God. We learn over time to have hope in God not in ourselves or not in people. Ultimately, God orchestrates everything, that's why it's especially important to develop a personal relationship by accepting Jesus Christ into your heart. It takes a while to get in rhythm with God, if you seek Him, He said He would be found *(Jeremiah 29:12-13 NKJV)*. What do I mean to get in rhythm with God? Some examples are being intentional to regularly flow with God by reading the scriptures, praying, being still by listening with the Holy Spirit's help, attending Spiritual classes so you're always growing; praising, and worshipping God (individually and corporately).

Chapter 11 – Me, My Kids, And Church
(Planting A Seed Early In Your Children's Lives)

I was around the age of 26 and decided to get back to church and seek after the Jesus my grandmother introduced me to many years ago at age 6. I needed that relationship my grandmother had. She had something special, and I was searching for it. The first church I remember attending with my daughters when they were young, made me feel really good. I felt like I was getting my life back on track. It was challenging, my children didn't want to go to church as much as I did. But I kept going because I needed Jesus to help me and my situation. It turned out that I would experience my first church hurt. It devastated me. The enemy comes, to steal, kill, and destroy, in all forms. *(John 10:10 NKJV)*

At this point in my life, I was minding my business and taking care of my children, I was not with their father and I was seeking God the best way that I knew how. The details are not important, but I was being pursued for an entire year by a gentleman and when I gave in my world came crashing down. After this, I had to pick myself back up again and start my process of healing all over again. You have heard them say, that what doesn't kill you makes you stronger. My God, did He make me stronger as my journey continued. My children finally got it that mom was going to go to church. I've heard them say today that they couldn't wait until they were older so they could stop going to church. How many times have some moms heard this? As our children begin to experience life, they find out how much they need a personal relationship with Jesus Christ.

Two of my children are serving in their local church. With the help of God, my children and I survived the early years when I attended church searching for the God of my grandmother. To God be the Glory! *(Proverbs 22:6 NKJV)*. If you're not attending church for whatever reason or you stop going to church, I encourage you to attend a good Bible-believing church with your family. If you need to go by yourself at the beginning, then you go by yourself and bring all of the love of God home with you and keep praying for your family. Or, if you're single go to church by yourself anyway. It will be okay, God said he'll never leave you nor forsake you *(Hebrews 13:5 NKJV)*. So, know that God is with you, you're not alone.

Chapter 12 – My Adult Daughters
(My Daughters Are True Survivors)

The saying "my adult daughters," is a joke that I say instead of saying "daughters," it makes my daughters laugh. My daughters are true survivors. I wanted to make sure that my daughters received an exceptional amount of love from me because of the trauma I experienced. I never wanted my daughters to have to go through what I went through. I taught them as much as possible when I could when we chatted.

After my first suicide attempt *(I have attempted suicide three times and I'm truly grateful that I'm still alive)* my daughters no longer lived with me. In addition to the experience, I didn't think I was going to make it without my daughters. I thought I would never have a relationship with my daughters again. My daughters were my world, and they are still my world. As God would have it in His sovereignty, I have an amazing relationship with all three of my daughters.

They were young at the time. For those that say, how could someone try to take their life when they have children or family or whatever the case. Let me tell you, if you've never been there, please don't be a judge. When you've lost all hope in your situation and think it will never get better from the lens of your eyes and the trick that the enemy plays in your mind. It's only by the grace of God that you make it. Unfortunately, I've heard of so many that have taken their lives to death by suicide. That's why I know that it was time for me to share my story and help in any way I can. I believe I heard the Spirit of the Lord say to me that I would be part of the solution to death by suicide. It was a long road back after my three attempts of suicide. My heart goes out to the many people that didn't make it. I think I'm qualified to say, that I know it has left a lot of questions in the minds of those that survived their family and friends who have taken their lives by suicide. I'm here to share that it was not easy for them to take their life. I know they thought long and hard before making the decision to take their life by suicide. It took many days for them to conclude to perform the act of suicide. The pain is so unbearable that you cannot see the hour, the minute, or the second in front of you. My prayers are with the family and friends of those who had someone to commit suicide.

Now that my daughters are adults their journeys are spiritual, and they have developed their own understanding of what it means to have a personal relationship with Jesus Christ. They have survived in different ways, so they are also survivors. I am so Godly proud of each one of them. They bring something different to this world and to others. They are very gifted and talented. Wow, I praise God for them, and they've found a way to express themselves in very unique ways.

My oldest daughter Maletta has a unique online boutique, my middle daughter Melony has a unique style to her painting business she shares with all ages, and my youngest daughter Maureen is creative in all types of ways, e.g., creating digital training modules to include her own voiceovers, etc. She has made her home an oasis of calm and peace. It's so amazing to see how God has blessed each of them!

My oldest daughter, Maletta permitted me to share this quick story ...

She called me crying one day saying that her son doesn't believe in God anymore. He was 18 years old at the time of this writing. After I listened to everything she was saying. She said she was going to put him out of her house.

I said you've done a great job raising your children from a natural standpoint. You gave them all the keys on how to be good kids, set goals, how to seek the things they want out of life. Now, you need to be a Spiritual mom. If you put him out, you'll be handing him over to the devil without a fight.

You have to start speaking to him from a Spiritual perspective. You have to fight for him in prayer. It's just not for him but it's for his children which are going to be your grandchildren. We need to fight in prayer for him. So, he'll become a man of God and lead his family into the things of God. I shared that's how they did it in the Old Testament, each one teach one.

After we hung up the phone, my prayer was, that someone who my grandson respected that is saved will help him to understand what it means to know

Jesus Christ personally. The Word of God says, that if we would plant a seed, another person would come by and water that seed, and God would bring the increase in that person's heart *(1 Corinthians 3:6-8 TLB)*. The growth in a person's heart is done by the grace of God and His supernatural power.

I didn't feel I should talk to my grandson right away. I was led to pray. Well, my middle daughter and I were talking, and the topic came up of my oldest daughter calling me and saying how she was going to put her son out of her house. My middle daughter shared with me that she was at my oldest daughter's house. It was just her and my grandson in the house after this happened. My grandson started talking to her. She was able to talk to him. I was believing God to bring the increase in my grandson's life in due season because my grandson already had the seed of God planted in him. We **must** fight for our families Spiritually. ***WE REALLY HAVE TO FIGHT FOR OUR FAMILIES AND FIGHT FOR THE CHURCH OF TODAY.***

When my grandson had a birthday in May 2022, I invited him out for a meal. I didn't remember right away, this incident that happened. When we got to the restaurant, I was reminded of my grandson no longer believing in God. I shared with him that you know your Nana is going to talk about God. It will not be all that we talk about, but you know your Nana. My grandson laughed. When the conversation about God and knowing Jesus Christ by having a personal relationship with Him was over, the Holy

Spirit had touched my grandson's heart. I didn't know to the extent my grandson was touched until I had lunch with his sister several days later for her belated birthday. The conversation came up and she shared with me that her brother said he was going back to church. That he said I had a talk with Nana. All I can say, is, God did it! God always uses people as His mouthpiece, hands, and feet to bring the good news, the Word of God. It was my grandson's appointed time to hear from God through his grandmother. This is the cycle of passing down Spiritual knowledge when you know Jesus Christ. And it's passed down from generation to generation. I'm so glad to be alive to witness the goodness of God and see how He miraculously answers our prayers.

Chapter 13 – My Continued Healing
(There's Destiny In Jesus Christ – I'm A Survivor)

When I hear of someone who has taken their life to suicide, I never forget the unbearable pain I was in, and I imagine the unbearable pain the person I hear about was in. I understand and don't pass judgment. It's terrible for everyone.

Being left to live after attempting suicide three times was a question in my mind for a very long time, although I am very thankful and grateful, I would ask God why I was left to live. I received the answer to this question only in the year 2022. I'm very big on leaving a Spiritual legacy for my children, grandchildren, great-grandchildren, and beyond. I understand how important this is and that's the answer God gave me. Because my grandmother was so instrumental in being sure I knew Jesus Christ, I always wanted to be like my grandmother in that respect. To be sure my children knew Jesus Christ for themselves. I knew that if they developed a personal relationship with Jesus Christ whatever they went through He would bring them through and out victoriously. Every chance I got when they would call me with a situation, I would immediately show them by example how to pray about it. I trusted that the best answer from the Lord would come to pass.

Even while still healing and winning my daughter's trust again, God was working on my behalf. God knew that I was confused for so many years. In His divine way, I was guided to Christian ministry classes where I received a couple of Christian ministry certificates. Praise God! I learned about having strongholds while taking a class, "Shattering Your Strongholds," by Alice V. Wilson. Ms. Wilson shared during the class that our outlooks, attitudes, and expectations are shaped by our experiences and reactions that started as far back as our early childhood. Many Christians have tried to leave the past behind by ignoring it rather than getting to the root. Have you ever asked yourself why am I the way I am? To heal past hurts, guilt, and unforgiveness, we need to allow the Holy Spirit to reveal the hidden areas of our hearts and to administer cleansing. If you are dealing with ongoing confusion or are plagued by endless doubt, anxiety, fear, lust, pride, bitterness, unforgiveness, and perfection – you are dealing with strongholds. Your strongholds may have enabled you to survive terrifying circumstances in your past that were out of your control. This is one of the reasons you trust them. But if they are still in place in your life, they are providing access [OPEN DOORS] for the enemy's assaults. They are also protecting wrong attitudes, beliefs, and patterns of thoughts you have learned to trust more than you trust the truth. You will find all of the above acts of the sinful nature (strongholds) in *Galatians 5:19-21 (TLB)*. Before learning these truths, I had been walking around for so many years like a zombie, not understanding what was happening to me. The so-called Walking Zombie Syndrome is described as a condition in which depression and withdrawal lead individuals to unconsciously believing that they were dead. After taking this particular class it enlightened me about strongholds, and I finally understood what was happening in my life. Emotional strongholds come in all shapes and sizes – anger, doubt, rejection, poor self-esteem, pride, stubbornness, a victim mentality, or defeatism. Harboring unforgiveness toward the person who was the source of my pain was taking a toll on my life. I eventually forgave the person.

Fannie Lou Hamer said, "I'm sick and tired of being sick and tired" and that was me.

Many years had passed before I started getting certified counseling and therapy. I, also, had hospital stays and other treatments to take me out of my deep depression. My sister was very instrumental in the beginning stages of helping me to get the help I needed. Again, certified counseling and therapy was not popular during this time. I'm so glad that since the pandemic, getting counseling and therapy is spoken of more freely. I encourage anyone to get what you need for your health and mental well-being. If people have never experienced what you are going through, they cannot be the judge or the jury of your life.

Whatever you are experiencing or have been experiencing I implore you to forgive. The pain from the hurt may not go away immediately, but if you give it over to God, He will take care of you and the situation. You may be wondering how do I give my situation over to God? You first need to receive Jesus Christ as your Lord and Savior. Be a member of a Bible-believing church and grow in God. In my experience of giving my situation over to God, in addition to having received Jesus Christ as my Lord and Savior and attending a Bible-believing church, I start by being in a quiet place in my home, focusing on the God I read about in the scriptures. I talk to the God that created the heaven and earth. The scriptures say … if you have faith as a grain of mustard seed … *(Matthew 17:20 NKJV)*. If you've ever seen a mustard seed, it is extremely small. I take my small faith at times and my giant faith at other times and trust and believe God can do anything but fail. I'm a witness that if you are experiencing the pain of a confused mind, God can heal you. It may not happen overnight, but some things that God is working on take time. Being in a good Bible-believing church will help in this transformation as you learn, grow, and receive the Word of God *(Romans 12:1-2)*. Also, participating in praise and worship services, I believe causes miracles and blessings to happen when believing in the God of the scriptures. You will not be able to get rid of the hurt and pain without having your own personal relationship with Jesus Christ the Son of God. He's the healer, He's the mind regulator, and He's whatever you need; *with men this is impossible; but with God all things are possible. (Matthew 19:26 NKJV).*

As a survivor of sexual abuse and mental health challenges, there is still destiny in Jesus Christ for my life. I can say this with Godly confidence. He has brought me through. My daughters and I have a very strong bond. I have beautiful grandchildren and great-grandchildren that I love, and they love me.

Me, my three daughters, and grandchildren have a lot of great talks about many topics. We still have bumps on the road, but we eventually work them out. I'm always sensitive in my Spirit; I never want to miss a moment where God can use me to help my family overcome obstacles and share God's wisdom and the tools He has given me. At times, I still need to ask for forgiveness. But no matter what, I always want to be emotionally present and available for my family.

This book is taking me out of my comfort zone to allow me to have a broader reach to help others. As a survivor of sexual abuse and mental health, there's truly destiny in Jesus Christ for your life. It all starts with having a personal relationship with Jesus Christ and being a part of a good Bible-believing church. Since we were created in God's image *(Genesis 1:27 NKJV)*. First Peter, chapter 4, verse 10 says, "Each one has received a gift, use it to serve one another as good stewards of God's varied grace" *(New American Standard Bible)*. This verse reminds us that the gifts we've been given are meant to be used for the benefit of others and to bring glory to God.

Chapter 14 – Making Self-Care A Priority
(Jesus Christ Practiced Self-Care)

I believe practicing self-care is biblical. Self-care can only be done well when you understand how much Jesus Christ cares for you, first.

It is not just about loving oneself but loving oneself so that we show off the glory of God to a world that needs to know Him.

In my opinion, Jesus Christ practiced self-care.

Throughout the New Testament, Jesus Christ took time to get away from the crowds to either rest or to spend time with our heavenly Father. Jesus Christ refueled by being still.

Everyone should take self-care very seriously, especially women. I try every three months, or every quarter, to be intentional about doing something for myself. Here are some examples for you, a staycation or by going to a local hotel to change your scenery, getting a massage, even if the massage is at a local mall where they have massage chairs. Also, using the chair massage function when getting a manicure and pedicure. Self-care can come in many forms, e.g., taking a nature walk, listening to the birds, bird watching, sitting on a balcony or deck clearing your mind, and eating at your favorite restaurant. Be creative and take yourself on a date when you're thinking of self-care. You can be married or single, it doesn't matter, you can take yourself on a date. I am single and I take myself on a date as often as I can. It's very refreshing and is one way to get refueled if your cup is running low. My personal goal is to do what I can to keep my cup filled and hope this will encourage you to not let your cup get empty.

To keep a personal relationship with Jesus Christ, you have to read the scriptures daily to cultivate the relationship and stay in the presence of the Lord Jesus Christ. It also helps your Spiritual growth to stay connected with your local Bible-believing church.

Keeping my cup filled is a part of self-care which I make a priority. Prayer is another priority and is a part of my self-care.

Here are very inexpensive and practical ways of taking care of yourself when you think about self-care.

- Do your own home Spa – some foot spas on the market have buttons that control the temperature of the water and provide bubbles which can be so refreshing. After your foot spa, massage your feet with a body souffle cream, or your favorite body oil or lotion. It's so refreshing. I found that different scents in the water of the foot spa can be very comforting and soothing.
- I would sometimes indulge in a foot spa while watching my favorite TV programs, which are westerns.

- I recently invested in a recliner that was on sale and has a heating and massage unit.
- I don't get on my stationer bike as often as I should, but I do fit it in also while I'm watching TV.
- Add vision boards to your surroundings. I know for a fact that items you post on your vision board do come to pass. You may say, what does a vision board have to do with self-care? It has a lot to do with caring for the future you desire by visualizing it with prayer and faith.
- Spiritual declarations that you say and that you look at often to meditate on help keep your Spirit up.
- If you're into water, walk around a lake to take in the scenery. You can always grab a jacket when the weather is cooler but don't let the weather stop you. I wouldn't go out in the rain.
- Men, I know you like to sit and watch football games how about tossing around a football with some young guys or playing flag football outside? How about going to a recreational center or the YMCA and playing basketball? Physical activity is rejuvenation.
- Having a positive mindset is self-care.
- Knowing your bandwidth is very important so you don't have an unexpected meltdown. What do I mean when I say bandwidth? Merriam-Webster defines bandwidth as "the emotional or mental capacity necessary to do or consider something? What is defined as a

"meltdown"? A meltdown is an intense response to an overwhelming situation. It happens when someone becomes completely overwhelmed by their current situation and temporarily loses control of their behavior. Living a life not knowing or understanding your bandwidth takes trial and error and will cause anyone to have a meltdown who has not figured this out and can cause your life to be very overwhelming. When I get to that point in my life where I sense my bandwidth is at its capacity and I feel a meltdown coming on, I look at my life and see what's on my plate and start eliminating some things because I realize I've taken on too much. I'm getting so much better at balancing my life. I encourage you to find the balance in your life. Philippians 4:11-13 says in verse 13, *I can do all things through Christ who strengthens me (NKJV)*. All things do not mean, you overload your life with busyness, etc. Your life has to be destiny driven.

- Discovering and finding self-care for yourself is refreshing, but it can sometimes take time.

Chapter 15 – It's A Win-Win With God
(The Power Of God)

When you incorporate Jesus Christ into your life by developing a personal relationship it's a win-win with God. If God is in your life and you understand that the very breath that you breathe comes from Him, you are headed in the right direction. God is our source, God is our everything, and God created each one of us. He gives us the use of our limbs in whatever capacity we find ourselves in. We are not to take God for granted. God is not our sugar daddy. He wants to have a real relationship with us. Why? Because He wants a family here on earth to be His hands, feet, and mouthpiece. God wants to partner with us here on the earth. To build His Kingdom, God does not want anyone to perish. This world we live in can be very harsh. The scriptures in the Bible is our guide to heaven as well as our instructions while living here on earth.

The power of God can save our souls and deliver us from sickness and diseases. But also, some of us will not get our healing until we reach heaven. Life is not always fair but having a relationship with the King of Kings and Lord of Lords, the great I am is a win-win. God can give you the peace you need to go through every day. The peace God gives is not peace that can be brought. It's supernatural that only comes from Him. While I was going through, I thought I would never make it out of the pain I was in. With the help of God, He got me through each day. I'm here to say, we serve a mighty God. He's Almighty!

He wants you to know that you can make it. He's
with you and He sees you. Take your life one day at
a time. If you can make it to a Bible-believing church
get there. His power and love will save you. I'm truly
a witness.

Chapter 16 – Giving God An Offering
(It's Not Always Monetary)

One of the churches I attended early in my Spiritual journey taught me about giving tithes and offerings unto God. Before I learned about giving my tithes and offerings unto God, I found out I was tipping God. Why do I say that? Because I was not giving from my gross income. Also, at this church, the Senior Pastor gave the members a challenge. If God does not bless you, you can take your tithes and offerings back. I was more interested in giving my tithes and offerings because I needed some things to happen in my life and I felt if I gave my tithes and offerings God would come through. I accepted the challenge. At a particular point in my accepting this challenge, I was praying for direction, I felt the Holy Spirit nudging me to downsize on the way I was living. I had been living on my own for some time. Granted I was only living in a one-bedroom, and I didn't have my children with me. This was going to be new for me as I thought about giving up my privacy and sharing space with someone. Thank God the person that was laid on my heart was Mrs. E. Taylor who is a very warm and caring woman who attended the same church. She agreed to me living with her. I shared about wanting to faithfully give my tithes and offerings and from there we established a good friendship. I am still friends with her today. I started tithing and giving my offerings. The many blessings that I have received from God has been amazing. I've shared my blessings with my family and others. It has been a great experience to be taught the importance of how God can use you to bless others and to get blessed. But ultimately, it's about being obedient to what God has called us as believers to do.

Giving God an offering is not always monetary. We can give of ourselves. You may wonder how we can give of ourselves. Volunteering at your local church and showing others the love of God is a major way to give God an offering. There's always a need for volunteers at the local churches. If you have gifts and talents, guess where they came from? Our God who created you, me, and the heavens and the earth. God wants to use us all. If you have a gift or talent and I'm sure you do, because you were created by God, help your church. If you haven't joined a church, what are you waiting for? You are needed in the Kingdom of God.

Giving God an offering can also take place outside the walls of the church. A major one for me, being kind to others. It costs nothing to give a smile. Pass the love of God onto others.

Chapter 17 – He Set Me Free!
(There Was Purpose In My Pain)

My freedom from my pain was a long time coming. I cried many nights and days for that matter wondering when this pain would be over. I cried out for deliverance on many occasions. God, please deliver me. I still worked and needed to support my family. It was hard but I remained in church. I was meeting new people on my Spiritual journey. I won't start naming people because I do not want to leave anyone out. The people that God had me to connect with were who I needed at the right time in my life. God is in control at all crossroads in our lives. You may not know you need this person or to attend a particular church, but God knows. The Holy Spirit will lead and guide you as you develop your own close relationship with the Heavenly Father. As I was coming to the end of my major deliverance, I mentioned how I was taking Spiritual classes at a particular church. One class that I attended taught us what it means to have strongholds and the need to forgive others. The class was so profound that after the class I immediately called the person who was supposed to protect me and finally said, "I forgive you." I found out that in that class the scriptures said that if you don't forgive that God would send the tormentors to you *(the person that would not forgive), (Matthew 18:21-35 NKJV)*. These verses talk about forgiveness. In my case, the person had moved on with their life. I walked around for years with an unforgiving heart which caused me a lot of unnecessary pain inside. It wasn't hurting the person;

it was hurting me. Destroying me on the inside. As the song says, killing me softly. I didn't know if I was coming or going but for the grace of God. I was never upset with God for what happened to me. When I would get in the presence of God worshipping His goodness and mercy, I would feel a release in my Spirit to keep going another day, then another day, then another day. It took many years of taking it one day at a time. I kept praying and crying out to God. Some days He felt so far away, other days He felt very near. I still have challenges, I am by no means perfect, but I've learned to trust God. I know that God can continue to help me to beat the odds for whatever challenges I will face. I finally was able to develop my own relationship with God the Father. I am so grateful that God's mercy endures forever, *Psalms 107:1 (NKJV)*. It wasn't until I forgave, that God gave me levels of freedom.

Now that I've matured, forgiven, and developed my own personal relationship with Jesus Christ, I know that the Holy Spirit placed in my heart to write this book. I had to say yes to this assignment and more importantly to have no more secrets. I understand that God wants me to help other women who may find themselves in similar situations or who are still keeping secrets that are destroying them on the inside. I'm a witness that God will get you through. Yes, by all means, protect your heart, but also think of others who may need to hear your story when you're healed.

Unfortunately, as women, we are not alone in suffering from different types of abuse. It's so important that women support one another. Yes, we've had different experiences, but at the end of the day, are our experiences so different? I'm saying yes to no more secrets. I've started this journey with my book, so if there's someone or another woman I can pray for or share my experiences with, in an effort that she can get better and have hope and be healed, so be it. I've said to the Lord, here I am, use me.

Chapter 18 – It Is So Important To Forgive Others

(There's Power In Forgiveness)

It is so important to forgive others because there's power in forgiveness. I harbored unforgiveness for many years and attempted to take my life on three occasions because the pain was so great. I overcame this tragedy by understanding the importance of forgiving others. I didn't know there was destiny in my life until years later. It came to me, that was the reason I was alive. I had destiny. God wanted to use me to save others from taking their lives to death by suicide or mental health challenges.

I made it a priority to love my children at the best level I could as well as being the best grandmother. I was given a second chance to show love. We've learned how people repeat family cycles, negatives, and positives. I didn't want to repeat the cycle of the hand that was given to me at such a young age. Instead of giving bitterness and hurt to my children and grandchildren, I gave an extra dose of love. I turned it around and loved my daughters at a level that I was not loved by the person who was supposed to love and protect me. I loved my grandchildren at this same level.

I understood after attending ministry classes that I had to forgive myself and forgive the person. That's what I did immediately, after understanding what strongholds meant in the scriptures. Again, I called the person and asked for their forgiveness. I learned that when I forgave, it was for me, not the person. This act alone started my healing process to include certified counseling and therapy. This act was not about reconciling with the person. In my opinion, reconciliation always has to be earned. In this context, I'm speaking of releasing offense against another person so I could move on with my life. In *Romans 12:17-21 The Message version says in verses 17-19, Don't hit back; discover beauty in everyone. If you've got it in you, get along with everybody. Don't insist on getting even; that's not for you to do. "I'll do the judging," says God. "I'll take care of it."* In the *Contemporary English Version, Mark 11:25-26, says, Whenever you stand up to pray, you must forgive what others have done to you. Then your Father in heaven will forgive your sins.* Over time as I matured in my walk with the Lord, I began to heal. Every day got better. I praise God to this day, that every day got better and is better.

If you harbor unforgiveness in your heart you can become stuck. If you have unresolved issues that you will not deal with, you'll be stuck and unable to move to your next level or any level. In my opinion, you can become sick which can possibly lead to bitterness, depression, and death by suicide. I don't want anyone to die of suicide that is within my reach by God's grace.

Here's a question from a quote I read that I want to ask you, "What is the power of forgiving others?" The answer: practicing forgiveness can have powerful health benefits. Forgiveness is associated with lower levels of depression, anxiety, and hostility. Forgiveness is associated with reduced substance abuse; higher self-esteem; and greater life satisfaction.

What I've learned over the course of my life, and I'm still learning, is that you must forgive yourself and those who have hurt you to receive the hope and healing you need. It was my responsibility to forgive myself and the person who allowed the sexual abuse, so I could move on with my life.

"To forgive is to set a prisoner free and discover that the prisoner was you." That quote comes from Lewis B. Smedes.

It was 1987, my first daughter was turning 10 years old, my middle daughter was 7 years old, and my youngest daughter was 3 years old. My oldest daughter was so happy, she was carefree and innocent, but as her 10th birthday approached. I became angry and depressed all over again. The person who was supposed to protect me, when I was 10 years old allowed me to be molested.

After the molestation happened, I would constantly ask the question, WHY did this person allow this to happen to me? I carried all that hurt in my heart, along with guilt, shame, anger, and not feeling like myself for years. Every time one of my three daughters turned 10 years old; I would remember the molestation. It was a delayed reaction of trauma. I was 10 years old, so I really didn't understand until I was older.

Many years had passed before I realized I needed counseling and therapy with what I was going through. I was in so much mental pain and didn't know how to describe it to anyone. I'm so glad our community is speaking out on mental illness, getting counseling and therapy, and not feeling ashamed. I still get counseling when I need it. Life does NOT stop life-ing. I go to church, I pray, and I read the scriptures. Because we need all the tools. The enemy does not want me to let you know that it's okay. He wants you to continue to feel guilty, to feel shame, and to be angry.

But, the *WORD of GOD* says, in *John 8:36 (KJV)*, whom the Son sets free is free indeed. *HIS* name is *JESUS*. *JESUS* wants everyone to be *FREE*. I believe the *WORD of GOD*. I had to get in a rhythm with my Heavenly Father in terms of going to church, praying, and reading the scriptures.

I cried out to my Heavenly Father for many years before I was delivered. I walked around not knowing if I was coming or going. My mind was NOT right. It was only the grace of God that allowed me to function from day-to-day and to hold down the jobs that I had. I praise *GOD* that I've worked for 31 years and retired September 30, 2021!!

I will never forget the scriptures that set me free *Matthew, chapter 18: verses 34-35 NKJV*.

v.34-And his master was angry and delivered him to the torturers until he should pay all that was due to him.

v.35-So My Heavenly Father also will do to you if each of you, from his heart, does not forgive his brother his trespasses.

Depression was eating me up on the inside, I would constantly get emotionally sick because according to Matthew, chapter 18, verses 34-35, I had not forgiven the person who allowed the molestation. After the Christian classes I was attending, that brought this revelation, I immediately left and called the person and said, "I forgive you." I felt it was my responsibility after understanding Matthew, chapter 18, verses 34 and 35 to forgive myself and the person so that I could move on with my life.

The quote from Fannie Lou Hamer says, "I'm sick and tired of being sick and tired" and that was me.

You can get stuck and *NOT BE ABLE TO MOVE ON* when you harbor unforgiveness. I'm definitely a witness to getting stuck, getting sick, and not moving on with my life while I was in my situation.

When you hold unforgiveness in your heart – it hinders your healing.

It's not always easy to forgive others, but with the help of Jesus Christ, we can make the decision to set the person or situation free in our heart. When we do, we also set ourselves free.

FORGIVENESS – has allowed me to have a very strong bond with my beautiful daughters, at this writing my oldest daughter is 46 years old, my middle daughter is 43, and my youngest daughter is 39 years old. I have 5 grandchildren, 2 grandsons who are 20, and 3 granddaughters in their 20's. And I have 3 great-grandchildren, ages 4, 3 and 1. I'm so *GODLY* proud of my family. My children's father passed away a few years ago. So, my girls and grandchildren do their best to love on me in their own special way. We have a lot of great conversations about life and just laugh a lot. I love it! Only Jesus Christ allowed my story to have a happy ending! *I AM SO GRATEFUL!!! TO THE GLORY OF GOD!!!*

FORGIVENESS – has allowed me to live a life of destiny. Sharing with you is one of my life's destinies and letting you know that whatever you're dealing with, it's okay. I live with mental illness *(specifically, a chemical imbalance, and it's okay)*. YES, it's okay. *TO GOD BE ALL THE GLORY!* HE keeps me covered with the *BLOOD OF JESUS*. I survived 3 suicide attempts. I don't know too many people who have survived 3 suicide attempts. *I GIVE ALL THE GLORY TO MY HEAVENLY FATHER!* So, be persistent in prayer and please don't give up on Father God. It's Critical.

FORGIVENESS – has allowed me to write this book. *TO GOD BE THE GLORY!*

FORGIVENESS – has allowed me to laugh more, I'm at peace with myself, and I'm enjoying my life.

~I BEAT THE ODDS~

I don't know what you're dealing with or what you have been dealing with for years, I don't know who hurt you, or what you're holding on to…I invite you to take that first step and decide to choose to forgive today, to start your healing. The Word of God says, in *Isaiah 53:5 (NKJV)* by Jesus' stripes, we are healed…Jesus Christ not only came to save us from sin, but He came to make us whole. Just like after understanding what the Word of God was saying in the book of Matthew, chapter 18, verses 34-35. I was responsible for what I did next. I had to make a choice. I could constantly be tortured because of unforgiveness in my heart or obey the Word of God and forgive. If you forgive yourself and those who've hurt you, you can begin the process of becoming a freer person, the Word of God says in *John 8:36 (NKJV), therefore if the Son makes you free, you shall be free indeed.*

You CAN become more focused; hope and healing unclutters your mind.

You CAN have more joy in receiving or renewing your relationship with the Lord Jesus Christ.

I BEAT THE ODDS, with the help of Jehovah-Rapha…my healer.

I BEAT THE ODDS, with the Lord Who Heals …
Physically-*2 Kings 5:10*

I BEAT THE ODDS, with the Lord Who Heals …
Emotionally-*Psalm 34:18*

I BEAT THE ODDS, with the Lord Who Heals …
Mentally-*Daniel 4:34*; and

I BEAT THE ODDS, with the Lord Who Heals …
Spiritually-*Psalm 103:2-3*

THERE IS HOPE AND THERE IS HEALING FOR YOU. IN JESUS NAME!!!

Chapter 19 – A Prayer Away
(God Loves You)

I want you to know that God cares for you and wants you to cast all your cares onto Him. *(I Peter 5:7 NKJV)*. My friend not only does God care about you, He sees you, but most importantly He loves you and wants the best for you. Please receive the love that our Father God has for you and begin your personal relationship with God through His Son the Lord Jesus Christ.

If you have not, please receive Jesus Christ as your Lord and Savior by praying out loud to our Heavenly Father the prayer below and confessing with your mouth and believing in your heart making Jesus Christ as the Lord over your life. It is that simple.

Romans 10:9-10 (New King James Version)

That if you confess with your mouth the Lord Jesus and believe in your heart that God has raised Him from the dead, you will be saved. For with the heart, one believes unto righteousness, and with the mouth, confession is made unto salvation.

Pray this prayer for salvation:

Dear Heavenly Father, I repent of my sins and ask you to forgive me. I confess with my mouth and believe with my heart that Jesus is your Son. I believe that Jesus died on the Cross at Calvary so that I might be saved from my sins. I believe that Jesus rose from the dead on the third day. I ask you right now to come into my heart and be my personal Lord and Savior. In Jesus' name. Amen.

If you have prayed this prayer with a sincere heart, mark this day as your born-again day! Please find a Bible-believing church so you may continue your Spiritual growth.

You may reach out to me at any time via email for further prayer at mwhitsett61@gmail.com.

Chapter 20 – Prayer Mapping
(Create Intimacy With God)

I am sharing prayer mapping as a consideration for those who have been believers for a while and desire to refresh their prayer life. By all means, do not neglect to continue to speak in the Holy Spirit which is our heavenly language not known to our enemy.

Background on mind mapping, a mind map is a visual representation of ideas and how they all relate to one another. The mind map begins with a central topic in the middle, and then new ideas can be added, moved, and connected to different ideas.

The history of mind maps can be traced back to the 3rd century. Mind mapping became popular around the 1970's when a British pop psychology writer named Tony Buzan introduced it on a BBC television show he hosted. Since then, mind mapping has been studied widely for its effectiveness in cognitive learning, memory retention, productivity, and creativity. People have been using mind mapping for years.

Mind mapping is used a lot in the corporate business world.

- Businesses and organizations have meetings and/or retreats to use mind mapping. They bond as a team when they're in this setting. Most importantly, they use mind mapping to plan out the upcoming quarters, years, or

- changes they want to make or to set strategic goals.
- Why can't you and I sit with God and do the same thing, but I'm calling it **prayer mapping** e.g., bonding with God, creating intimacy, and planning out our lives? Write the vision and make it plain. *(Habakkuk 2:2-3 NKJV)*
- This is a way to give intentional thought to the way we pray. By turning what some of us may do on our corporate jobs into something Spiritual that builds our prayer lives.
- I used mind mapping on my job when I was working on many occasions to help me see visuals of what was in my head.
- I felt a need to start prayer mapping to help me have a more intentional prayer life, and fresh prayers, and to get more intimate with our Father God. Prayer mapping also allowed me to visually see when God answered my prayers, and I could keep a record of them. I'm expecting God to answer my prayers and I can track them when using Prayer Mapping.

Prayer mapping is fun for me, it boosts my creativity, and prayer mapping has boosted my prayer life. I believe in my heart that it can enhance your prayer life.

Let me share a few reasons why prayer mapping is fun but serious and boosts your creativity.

Prayer mapping helped me to have an intentional prayer life.

Some of the tools that helped me have an intentional prayer life are:

- Asking the Holy Spirit to be with me before I start studying and reading the scriptures
- Studying different versions of the Bible
- Reading Commentaries *(just to see what others are saying but sticking to the Word of God, of course)*
- Pulling out Lyrics in Christian songs
- Searching the scriptures that line up with the lyrics in a song *(you'll begin to see the songs differently)*
- Reading Spiritual Books
- Meditating on God's Word
- Journaling my prayers to pray

If you do or do not have a prayer life, consider refreshing or starting your prayer life.

- You will build on your prayer life as you continue to meditate on God's Word.
- Our prayers should not be all about give-me, give-me, give-me.
- Our prayers for example should:
  - Talk to our Heavenly Father of the magnitude He is in our lives,
  - Show gratefulness,
  - Tell our Heavenly Father how much we love and need Him, and

o Always thank Him for what He has and is already doing in your life.

Below is an example of Spiritual Prayer Mapping that has helped me to create intimacy with God:

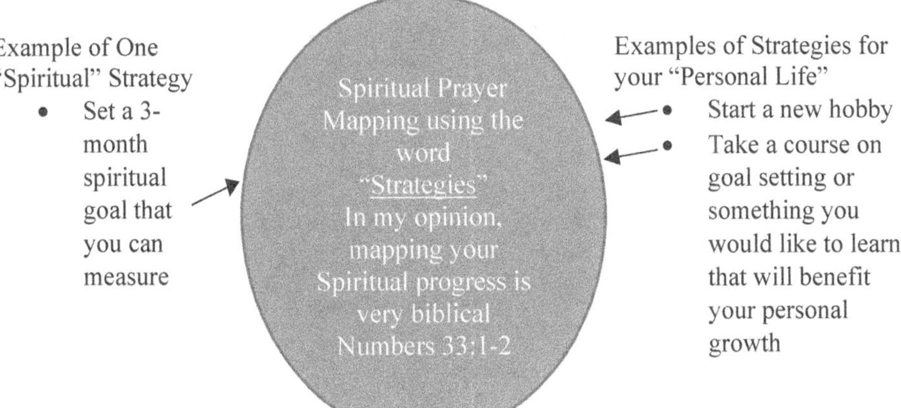

Example of One "Spiritual" Strategy
- Set a 3-month spiritual goal that you can measure

Examples of Strategies for your "Personal Life"
- Start a new hobby
- Take a course on goal setting or something you would like to learn that will benefit your personal growth

After setting up your prayer map you would simply spend time with God praying over everything you listed. Prayer mapping can be used for individual people you want to pray over, groups of people, such as families, or using just words to encourage yourself, don't put any limits on what our Father God can do.

God said His Word would not return void. *(Isaiah 55:11 NKJV)*. When you add scriptures to every prayer point your end results are:

- Having intimacy with God or building your relationship with God because you're giving

God back His Word as you pray and talk to Him.

- You're showing your gratefulness or gratitude as you thank God when He answers your prayers.
- You're creating a visual record or map of prayers prayed and prayers answered.

Chapter 21 – Your Story Is Still Being Written
(You Can Do It!)

There's hope and healing for you, you can do it, that's why your story is still being written and so is mine. If you're still breathing, which you are because you're reading this book, God has not given up on you. Every day you wake up is a new day to write your story. It's a new day to do something you've never done before. It's another day to get a second, third, fourth, or even a fifth or more chance at life. It's an opportunity to start over. You can do it! If I beat the odds, so can you. God is no respecter of persons, if He does it for one, He can do it for another. *(Acts 10:34 NKJV).*

I want to encourage you to write your own story of how you have or will beat the odds that are in your life. I know there is something you can write about. If you have nothing to write about at this moment and you are just getting started on your journey of hope and healing, I encourage you to write about the new journey you want to see and seek God's guidance and direction.

Along with starting to write your own story, you can start your vision board of what you want to see come to pass in your life. Start praying over these tools you're creating for your life. Stick with it, be consistent, write, pray, seek the presence of the Lord. Ask the Holy Spirit to lead, guide, and direct your path in all that you're about to do or continue to do,

in the name of the Lord. If you need prayer, you can
always reach out to me at:
                    mwhitsett61@gmail.com.

If you do not have a church home, seek out a Bible-
believing church and start your membership.

Chapter 22 – I Beat The Odds
(And So Can You!)

As I have shared my story, I want you to know how most women are not that different. I beat the odds with the mercy and grace of God and I know there's hope and healing for you too.

The last thing that I remember about my biological father is that he was an alcoholic and an abuser, but I am neither an alcoholic nor an abuser, *I beat the odds.*

Because I was a victim of childhood sexual abuse, I developed anxieties, depression, and mental health challenges. With the help of God, He has and is still healing me, *I'm beating the odds.*

Because I was a victim of childhood sexual abuse, I formed misguided interpretations of the world and relationships, now I'm okay with how I see the world and relationships because of God, *I beat the odds*.

I was able to graduate from high school just before I gave birth to my first daughter, *I beat the odds.*

I had my first child at age 16, yes, I was a teenage statistic, but I didn't stay there; *I beat the odds*.

I was on public assistance for a season but didn't stay there; *I beat the odds*.

I was able to take some college courses over the years even though I never received a college degree, but a master's degree in life; *I beat the odds*.

I was able to get into a program that placed me in a federal government position upon successful completion of the program; *I beat the odds*.

I left the federal government after three years because I didn't understand the politics but was able to return when I did understand the government's benefits; *I beat the odds*.

I have retired from the federal government after 21 years of service and 11 years in the private sector; *I beat the odds.*

I made a six-figure salary when working for the federal government; *I beat the odds*.

I've accomplished a lot while dealing with mental health challenges, that's why I know without any doubt there's hope and healing for you too. To God be all the glory for the great things he has and is still doing! *I'm beating the odds*.

Although I take depression medication every day, my chemical imbalance has long been in remission; *I'm beating the odds.*

I beat the odds, so I can touch one life at a time. To God Be All The Glory!
You can reach out to me for more valuable resources at: mwhitsett61@gmail.com

~I BEAT THE ODDS~

P.S.

To the men reading my book, I encourage you to purchase copies for your sisters, female families, and female friends. You may not know what they may be experiencing. I know my book will give them a source of hope. If I can beat the odds, God can help others to beat the odds. Please give other females a chance to experience God's love. He loves us all. Amen!

P.P.S.

Through my church which covers me, I was able and blessed to receive approximately 18 hours of life-changing and life-giving personal ministry. The personal ministry had a tremendous impact on solidifying my healing and gave me added tools for my continued Spiritual journey to freedom in Jesus Christ with the ability to live in faith, to put all my hope, and trust in Father God. To God be all the Glory!

APPENDIX

Links To Various Organizations to Assist With Child Sexual Abuse, Mental Illness, And Trauma
(These are not exhaustive)

National Association of Adult Survivors of Child Abuse
http://www.naasca.org/2016-articles/103116-factsheet-statisticsofchildsexualabuse.htm

Crime Victims Center (empowering victims & crime prevention)
https://www.parentsformeganslaw.org/statistics-child-sexual-abuse/

U.S. Department of Health & Human Services, Children's Bureau, an Office of the Administration for Children & Families
https://www.acf.hhs.gov/cb

Journal of Pediatric Psychology
https://www.ncbi.nlm.nih.gov/pmc/articles/pmc2722133/

National Institute of Mental Health | Transforming the Understanding and Treatment of Mental Illnesses
https://www.nimh.nih.gov/health/publications/fact-sheets

Center for Mental Health Services (CMHS)
https://www.samhsa.gov/about-us/who-we-are/offices-centers/cmhs
-95-

The UCLA-DUKE University National Center for Child Traumatic Stress (NCCTS)
https://www.nctsn.org/about-us/structure-and-governance/national-center

The National Child Traumatic Stress Network (NCTSN)
https://www.nctsn.org

Before You Go…

Thank you so much for reading *I Beat The Odds, There's Hope and Healing For You.* My prayer is that this book encourages your heart and reminds you that you are not alone.

If this book blessed you, would you take a moment to leave a review on Amazon?

Your review helps others who may be searching for hope and healing find this message.

Thank you for your support and for being part of this journey.

With love and gratitude,
Maureen Whitsett

Leave your review here:
(https://www.amazon.com/dp/B0GV4JCMQQ)